To the beginning
of a new path!
Love,
Numzy ♥

SHOOT FOR THE MOON.
EVEN IF YOU MISS IT
YOU WILL LAND AMONG
THE STARS.

New days, new life for you,
and I wish you the best
in this new way
        Kisses
              Delphine

PETER PAUPER PRESS, INC.
WHITE PLAINS, NEW YORK

PETER PAUPER PRESS
Fine Books and Gifts Since 1928

Our Company

In 1928, at the age of twenty-two, Peter Beilenson began printing books on a small press in the basement of his parents' home in Larchmont, New York. Peter—and later, his wife, Edna—sought to create fine books that sold at "prices even a pauper could afford."

Today, still family owned and operated, Peter Pauper Press continues to honor our founders' legacy—and our customers' expectations—of beauty, quality, and value.

Cover text by Les Brown

Designed by Heather Zschock

Copyright © 2005
Peter Pauper Press, Inc.
202 Mamaroneck Avenue
White Plains, NY 10601
All rights reserved
ISBN 978-1-59359-380-3
Printed in China
56 55 54 53 52 51

Visit us at www.peterpauper.com